BOOK 1

EARLY INTERMEDIATE PIANO

ROMANTIC SKETCHES

12 DELIGHTFUL SOLOS IN ROMANTIC STYLE
MARTHA MIER

The solos in *Romantic Sketches*, Book 1, will delight pianists who favor the Romantic style. Playing with musical expression is an important skill used in "making music," and is much more than just playing the notes on the printed page. Music written in the Romantic style is the perfect choice for developing this skill. These short, musical sketches will encourage students to play with nuance and sensitivity.

Romantic Sketches, Book 1, is sure to be a delightful milestone in your musical journey.

Enjoy!

Martha Mier

CONTENTS

Alfred

ISBN-10: 0-7390-4634-9
ISBN-13: 978-0-7390-4634-0

Starlight Prelude

Martha Mier

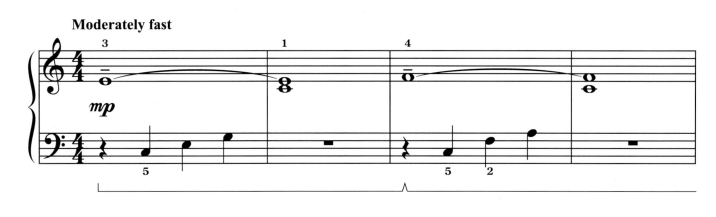

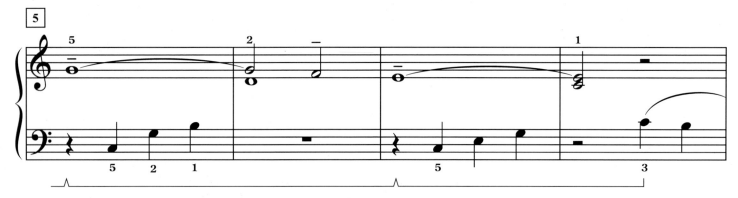

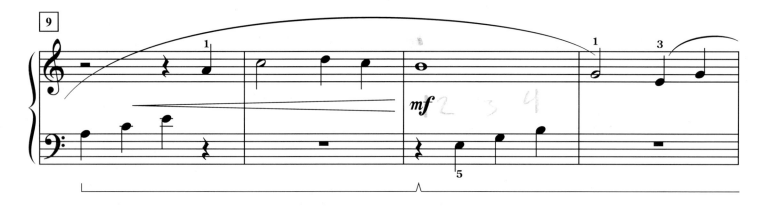

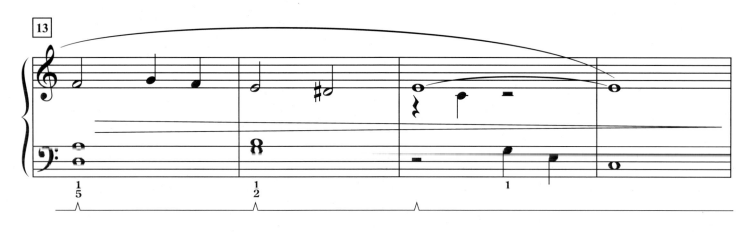

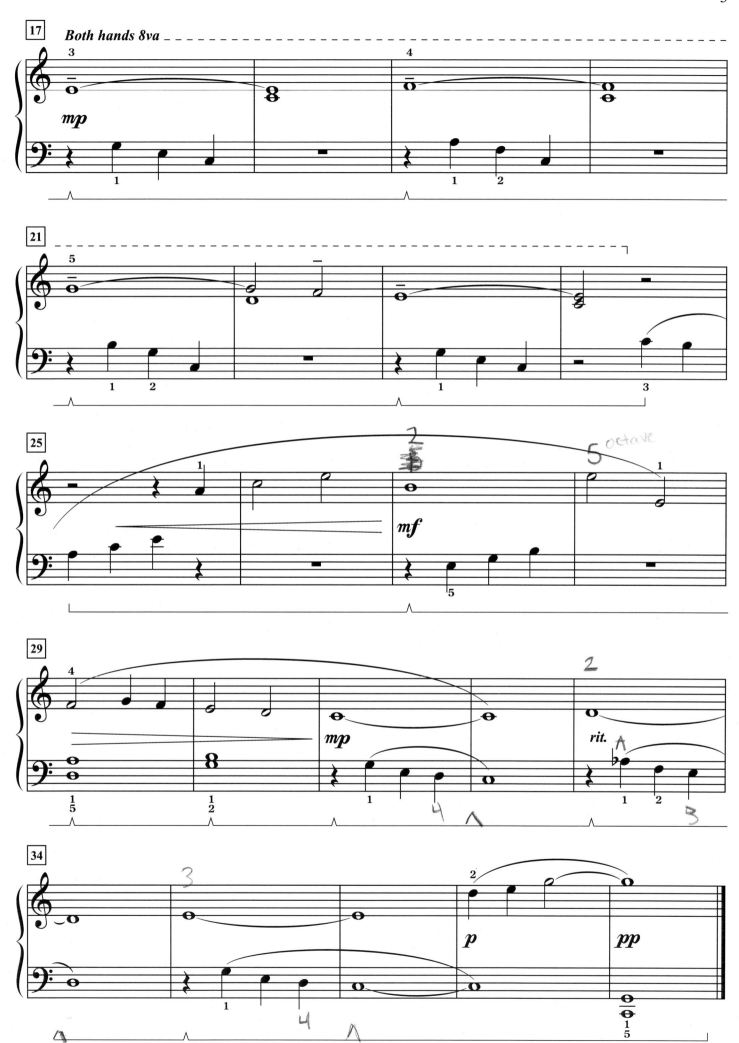

Medieval Festival

Martha Mier

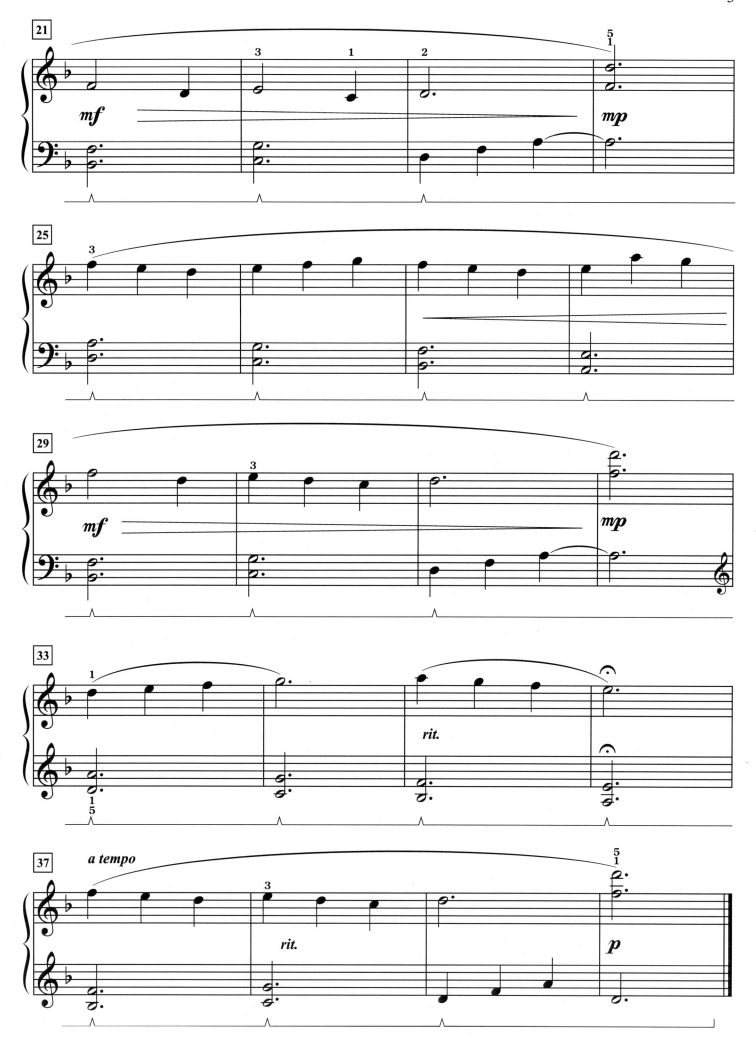

LITTLE SONG

MARTHA MIER

A Story from Long Ago

Martha Mier

Special Moments

Martha Mier

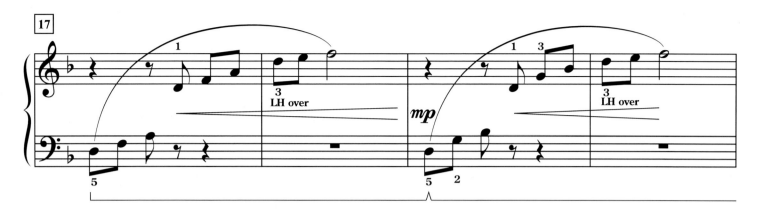

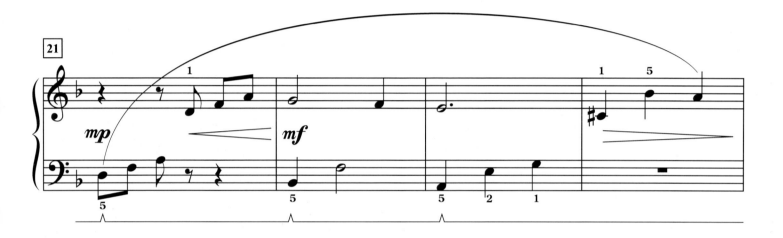

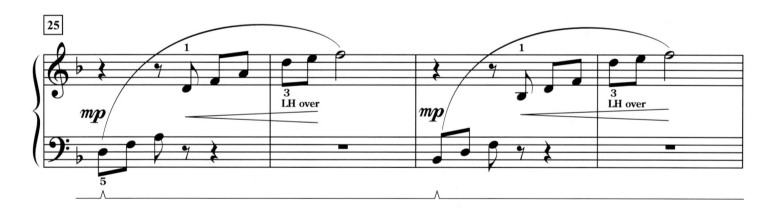

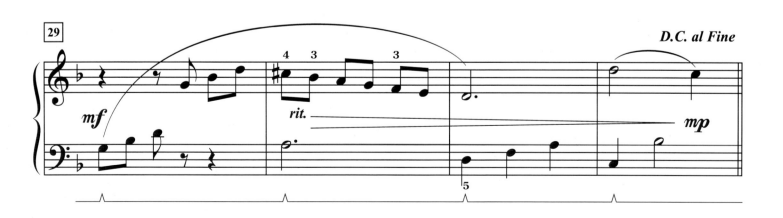

PROMISES

MARTHA MIER

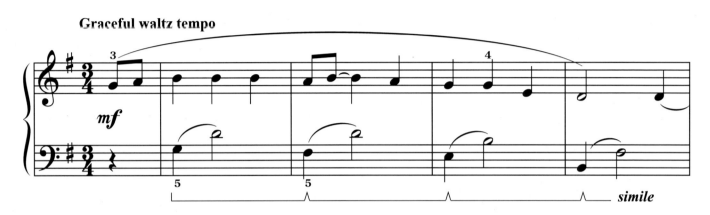

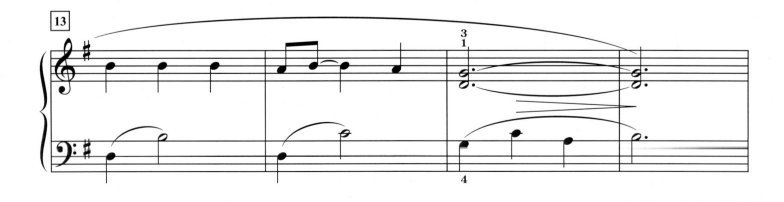

Morning Light

Martha Mier

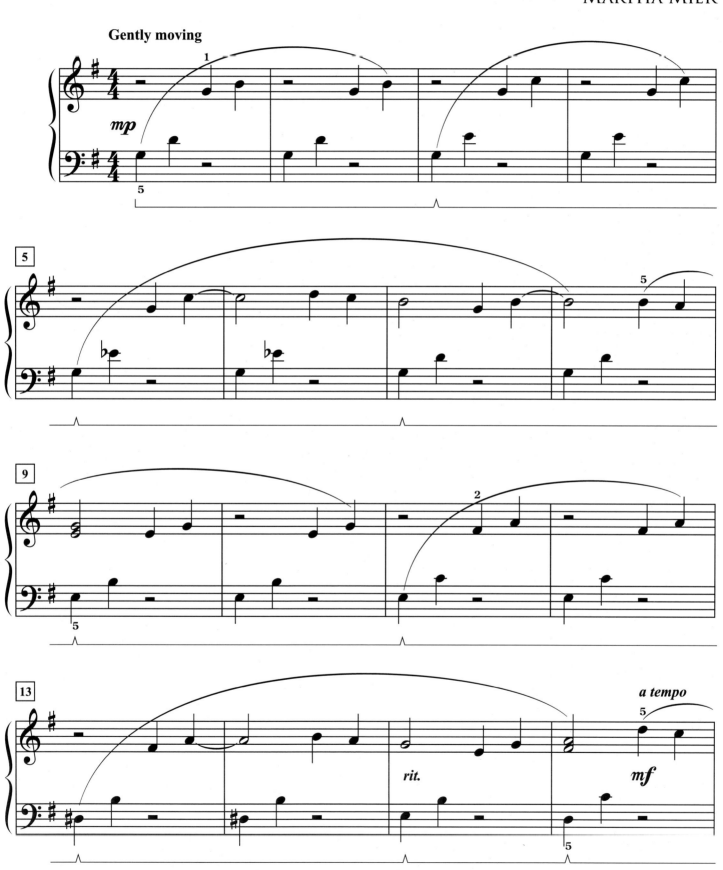

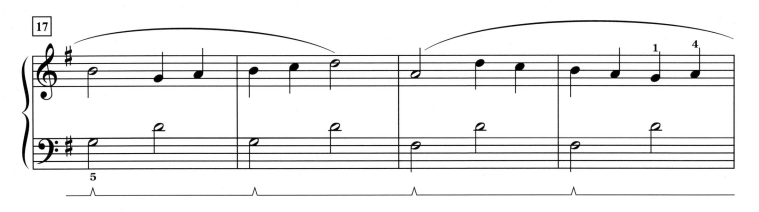

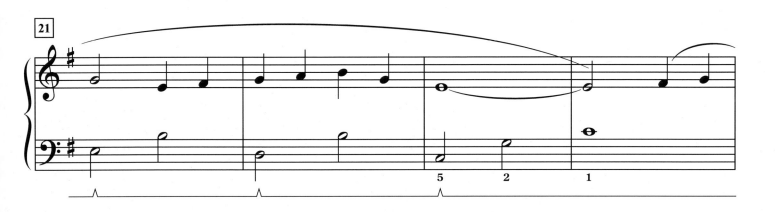

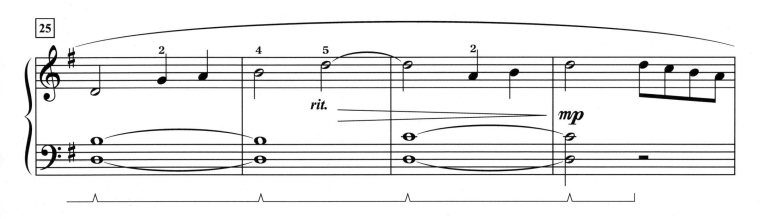

THE PERFECT ROSE

Martha Mier

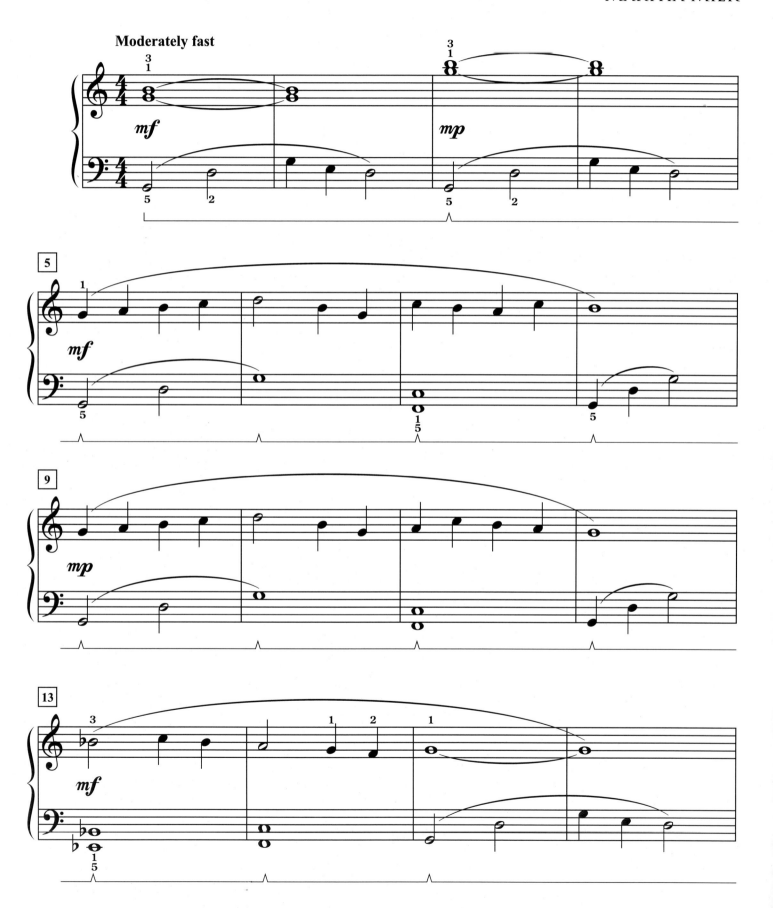

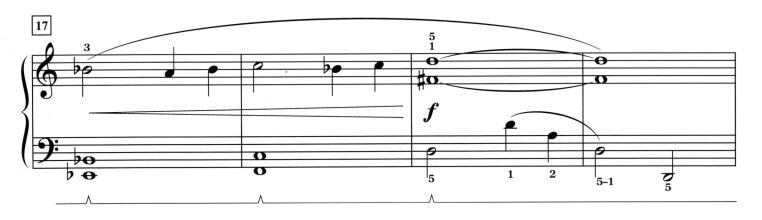

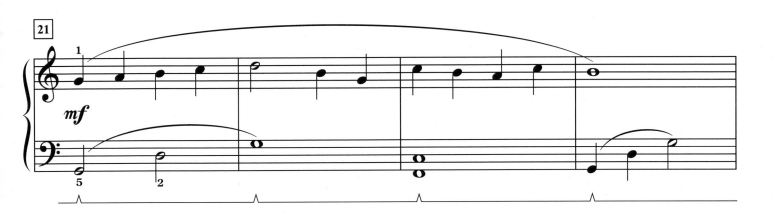

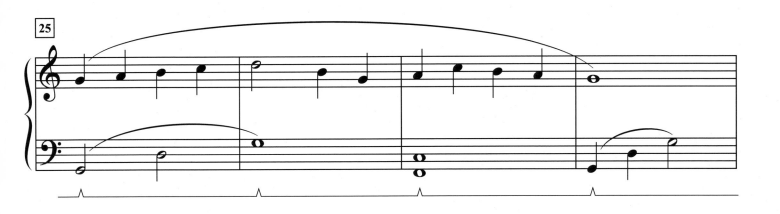

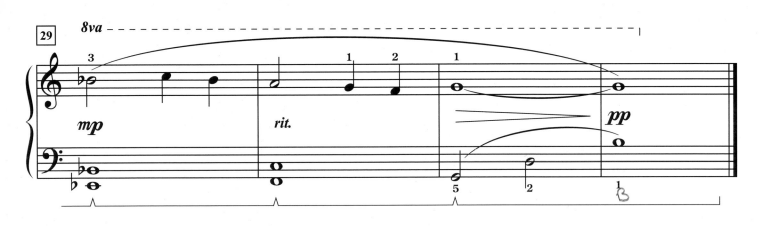

A Fond Farewell

Martha Mier

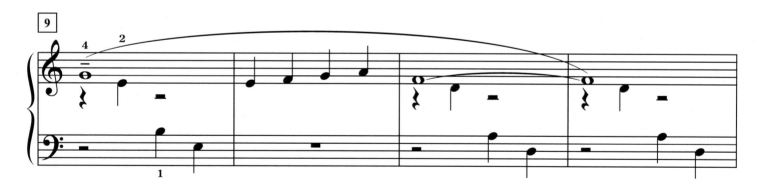

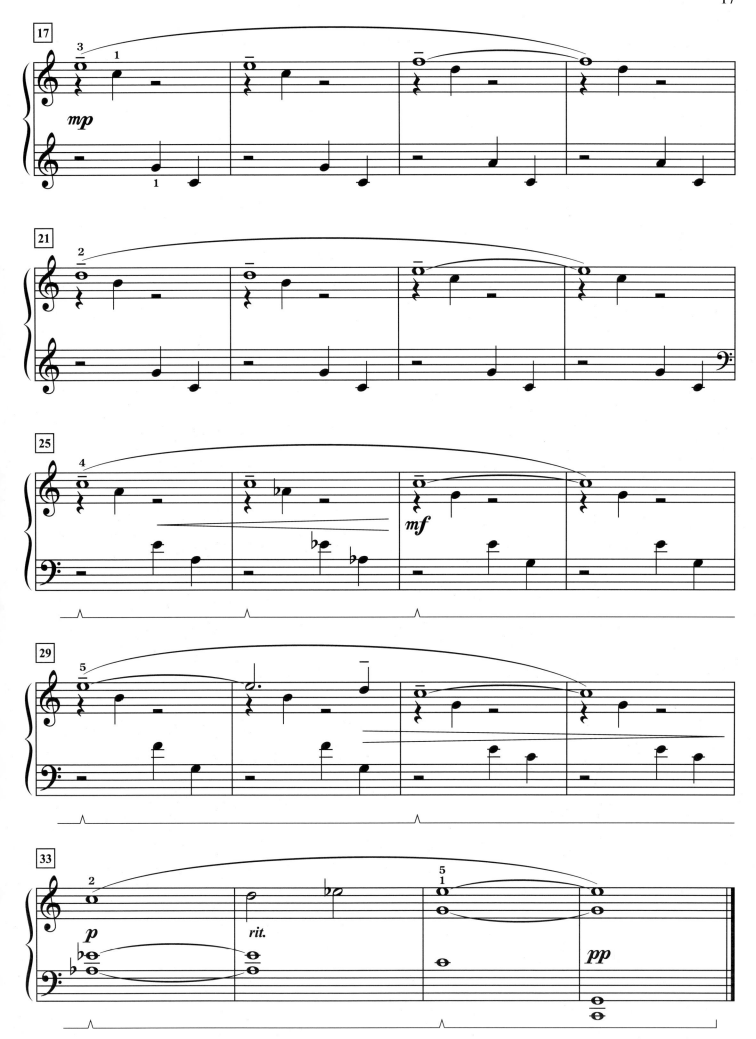

Summertime Waltz

Martha Mier

Moderately fast, with excitement

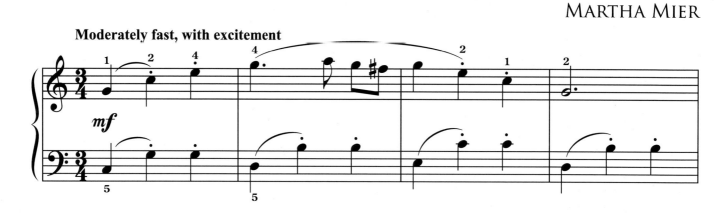

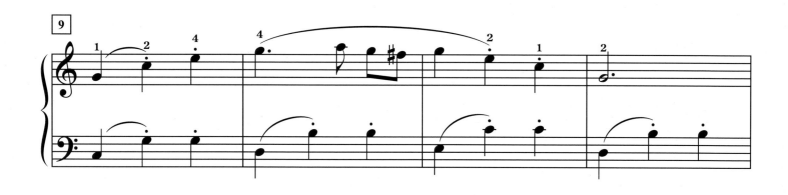

SHADOW DANCE

MARTHA MIER

Sun Showers

Martha Mier